"True"
Tall tales of
old Vermont

Retold by

Harold A. Wilkinson

Original artwork by

Francis Hinkley

First edition, 2005

Second (expanded) edition, 2009

Order this book online at www.trafford.com
or email orders@trafford.com

Most Trafford titles are also available at major online book retailers.

Note for Librarians: A cataloguing record for this book is available from Library
and Archives Canada at www.collectionscanada.ca/amicus/index-e.html

Printed in Victoria, BC, Canada.

ISBN: 978-1-4269-1589-5

*Our mission is to efficiently provide the world's finest, most
comprehensive book publishing service, enabling every author to
experience success. To find out how to publish your book, your way, and
have it available worldwide, visit us online at www.trafford.com*

Trafford rev. 9/11/2009

 www.trafford.com

North America & international
toll-free: 1 888 232 4444 (USA & Canada)
phone: 250 383 6864 ✦ fax: 812 355 4082

Contents

Introduction

Fred Bernard was a true Vermonter. I do not know when his family first came to live in southern Vermont in the Whitingham-Wilmington area, but it may have been not too long after the first permanent European settlers arrived. These settlers came to this pleasant valley after the end of the French and Indian wars made it safe enough for Europeans to live in the Green Mountains, a generation or so before the Revolutionary War. In any event, Fred had lived all his life here, and when I first met him he had been living here-- and collecting the stories he loved to tell-- for some eight decades

We built our second home in lovely southern Vermont as a refuge from the hectic and "high tech" urban environment, as a place to rediscover the beauty and peacefulness of nature and as a focal point for enjoyment and togetherness for our growing family. Discovering Fred Bernard and his stories of old Vermont was an unexpected and happy bonus. Meeting Fred and listening to his tales added to our sense of identity with our adopted second home and became one of the truly memorable aspects of our experience in Vermont. Through Fred we came to know more personally the rugged New England spirit which motivated these hardy people and kept them vigorous through the hardships of the long New England winter and the tribulation of mud and black flies which is called "Spring." Because these tales have meant so much to me, I hope that sharing them with others will bring to them also a sense of the joy of living which this vibrant man so casually shared with me.

I met Fred Bernard by accident and through the unlikely intermediary of a half cord of hardwood. On the recommendation of neighbors I ordered firewood from Fred Bernard in time for our first winter in Vermont, which I was anticipating as a long and cold experience. The firewood arrived in a battered pick-up truck on a gorgeous Fall afternoon, with the bright sunlight causing the fabled Vermont Fall foliage to glow vibrantly and gloriously. Unexpectedly the battered pick-up truck contained something even more lasting for me in its warmth than the hardwood: a jovial Vermont octogenarian named Fred Bernard. On the day of that first delivery, and with each subsequent delivery, with the firewood came-- always free of charge!-- lively tales about bygone times in southern

Vermont. Fred recounted these yarns always with gusto and he guaranteed that each and every one of them had actually happened! I soon learned that Fred's real talent was not cutting and splitting wood, but spinning yarns and recounting a vivid chapter of Vermont's history which somehow has failed to reach the learned history books-- though they speak volumes about the rugged people who live in Vermont. Fred's skill, which may be on its way to becoming a "lost art", was the art of historical recounting through storytelling. But the tales Fred told were not the stories of battles, politics or major governmental upheavals. Rather, the tales Fred told were the stories of real people struggling to survive and to better themselves.

At first Fred brought the wood himself, but in those earlier days of our acquaintance he was younger, vigorous and only 80 or so years old!

Storytelling time in those days came after the firewood had been taken off of his truck and stacked in a neat pile and during that time of relaxation while the bill was being paid. Over the next decade time began taking its toll, so that Fred would arrive with the firewood accompanied by his daughters and granddaughters. Watching them and helping them unload and stack the firewood allowed even more time for spinning yarns, which Fred obviously always loved to do. Unfortunately I never wrote down the tales Fred told, and even more unfortunately Fred is no longer with us to regale us in his usual hearty manner. I will never forget those pleasant times spent with Fred, but unfortunately I have forgotten many of his tales. Unfortunately also I will not be able to recreate the actual scene of the firewood delivery, with Fred in his overalls lounging against his battered pick-up truck against the backdrop of the brilliant Vermont

Fall foliage, nor will I be able to capture the artfulness of Fred's droll and colorful delivery of his tales. Nevertheless the tales that I do remember humorously evoke an image of Vermont life in the early 20th century which I would like to share with my readers. Maybe by trying to retell his tales I'll help a little to keep alive the sense of joy in living that Fred transmitted so memorably to me.

I am indebted to one of Fred's nephews, Mr. Arnie Bernard, for his help with the expanded, second edition of this compilation of tales. In the course of several pleasant chats, he was able to come up with several more of Fred's tales, and I have included them in this expanded second version of this literary effort. I am also indebted to a very clever artist I have known for many years, Mr. Fred Hinkley. His humorous drawings add considerably to this effort.

Brotherly love
has its limits

Fred was the oldest of seven children and inherited French and some Indian blood from his parents. Being raised on a farm in rural Vermont, Fred's family was a tight knit group who cared strongly for each other and who always vigorously defended each other when and if the need arose.

But being the oldest of the five boys, Fred felt a particular need to look out for his younger brothers and to help direct them. He was not only the oldest boy, but he was the biggest -- and the other four conceded that he was also "the meanest." When he was alone with his brothers, Fred tended to "rule the roost," and he always seemed to have strong ideas about what needed to be done and how it should be done.

As was the custom in those days, all of the children were expected to pitch in to help run the farm and household and to help with the family business, and all of them did so vigorously. Since their father himself was a wood cutter of some renown in the region, he had a brisk business supplying firewood to neighbors near and far. As soon as the boys were big enough and strong enough to help with the work, they too were dispatched into the woods to help with cutting trees and turning them into firewood.

When they became a little older, the five boys would be sent out into the woods as a team with Fred in charge and no grown-ups around. Even as a young man Fred knew the wood cutting and firewood business well, and he was always confident about what needed to be done and how it should be done. He took charge of his team of brothers conscientiously and vigorously. Perhaps it was partly because he was, after all, only their older brother, his brothers found his leadership skills to be rather abrasive and annoying. Even though he seemed always to be right, it wasn't always easy for his brothers to accept that fact.

One day in the woods, the brothers felled a particularly large rock maple tree. Fred issued orders to his brothers in his usual gruff and somewhat impatient way, then set about "limbing" the fallen tree, cutting off the limbs and deciding whether some of the larger ones might be useful for making firewood. The brothers watched as he stood beside the tree trunk below a large branch which jutted out from the trunk to the side and upward at a steep angle, leaving a tight fork between the trunk and the limb. He had his back turned to them, and they quickly conferred in whispers about a plan of action. Rushing up behind Fred, they grabbed him by the seat of his overalls and dumped him headfirst into the fork of the tree, where he wedged fast! Fred howled and swore that retribution would be swift and ferocious -- but he was stuck tight. Anger quickly turned to laughter and the brothers lifted Fred out of his predicament. Brotherly love had won out, and Fred had heard loud and clear the message that he needed to improve his management skills.

Looks can be deceiving

Fred was a crafty fellow and a good businessman, but he didn't care much about appearances. There were certainly special days on which he needed to wash up and dress up, but for the most part he was content with his worn and baggy bibb overalls and his comfortable flannel shirt. He tended to dress in this fashion year-round, summer and winter, and nobody who knew Fred objected or thought this was anything but proper.

Fred had grown up in hard times, and he was always careful with money. It was said that, "he still had the first dollar he ever earned." Fred worked himself hard, and he worked his farm equipment and pickup trucks equally hard. Being both crafty and frugal, he felt that he got the best return for his money if he always bought a good truck, and a new truck at that, whenever the old one wore out. For years he had bought his trucks from "Doc" Roberts, who owned the business near his home in Whitingham.

Being frugal as well as crafty, it didn't escape Fred's attention when he heard that a new truck dealership had opened up over the mountain in Brattleboro and was offering to sell trucks more cheaply than "Doc" Roberts did. So when the day came that his pickup truck was near to breathing its last, Fred decided to take advantage of what sounded like a good deal and make the trip over the mountain.

He found the new dealership to be housed in an elegant and flashy new building festooned with flags and balloons. The dealer was dressed in a natty suit with a clean white shirt and a flashy necktie. Of course Fred was dressed in his usual attire, his baggy and worn bibb overalls and flannel shirt. The dealer greeted Fred with a handshake and listened as he described the type of pickup truck he wanted to buy. He took Fred to a lot behind the building and began showing him used trucks. Fred protested, and carefully explained that he wanted to buy a new pickup, not a used one. Somewhat condescendingly the dealer undertook to explain to Fred that those shiny new trucks parked in front of the building were pretty expensive, but that he could offer Fred a used pickup at a much lower price. Even though Fred protested, the dealer seemed skeptical that Fred could afford such a luxury. Fred liked a bargain when he could get one, but he had a strong sense of pride, and now his pride had been trampled upon.

Fred promptly left the Brattleboro dealership and drove back across the mountain to see old "Doc" Roberts. He found just the pickup truck he wanted in "Doc" Roberts' lot. After negotiating the price, Fred reached into the pocket of his overalls, pulled out a fat roll of green bills and peeled off just enough cash to pay for the truck. It's too bad the other dealer looked only at Fred's clothes.

Selling firewood:
the customer always
knows best

Fred Bernard began cutting, splitting and selling firewood many years ago. He always prided himself on providing his customers with only the best wood, carefully dried, and always in full and honest measure. There was plenty of wood in Vermont, but turning a full grown hardwood tree into several cords of prepared firewood required a lot of work, a lot of sweat and a lot of calluses. A man who could do this work well could take pride in his work, and Fred was no exception. Fred knew firewood. And he knew his customers, all of whom were neighbors. And Fred had been raised right, and he knew the value and importance of honesty and neighborliness.

One of his steady customers, whom we will refer to as "Miss Ettie" (as Fred referred to her), regularly ordered two cords of firewood each winter to heat her small house. But she was very particular about the kind of wood she ordered. Each time she stipulated that it must be poplar or white birch wood. Now both poplar and birch are "soft" woods and burn up quickly, without the lasting and long burning quality of "hardwoods." No wonder it took so much wood to heat such a small house!

Fred tried to explain this to Miss Ettie, being a good neighbor as well as a businessman. If she would burn good Vermont hardwood, she could probably heat her house all winter with half the amount of wood-- and at half the cost. But Miss Ettie could not be convinced or dissuaded, and dismissed Fred's careful explanations with a firm, self-righteous and ladylike wave of her hand. She was accustomed to being right, and her children and grandchildren all knew that she was right and was the final authority in the family. In her turn she tried to get Fred to understand that the poplar and birch wood, "Looked a whole lot nicer."

Fred felt bad about this because he knew that Miss Ettie was an elderly widow and did not have a lot of money, and he felt she was wasting her money on inferior firewood. He had given up trying to persuade her, but after much deliberation he decided to try to be helpful in a rather indirect way. The next time he delivered a cord of firewood to Miss Ettie's house he included four solid sticks of high quality, long burning hardwood along with the poplar and birch wood. He figured that if she would just try burning a few sticks of hardwood she would soon see the difference. As usual, Miss Ettie watched carefully from the window of her small house as Fred unloaded and stacked the firewood.

After he had finished Fred sat down for "a breather" and waited to be paid. When Miss Ettie came out and inquired about the price, Fred told her that the price would be $8, as usual. She nodded, and Fred waited patiently while she went back into her house, knowing that she always paid on the spot and in cash. Soon she returned and handed him seven dollars and 80 cents. Fred was greatly surprised and pretty flabergasted, because Miss Ettie always paid her account in full and was always very careful about the amount. He was a bit embarrassed as well and stammered, "But Miss Ettie, I just told you that the wood cost eight dollars. You have paid me 20 cents short." Triumphantly she drew herself up to her full height-- still a full head shorter than

Fred--, looked up at him and announced, "That's exactly right, Fred Bernard. We agreed that I would pay you eight dollars for a full cord of good wood. Don't think that I didn't see you slip in those four sticks of old ugly wood! I have no intention of paying you for that no good wood and you can just take it back home with you!" With that she turned and majestically and with righteous indignation strode back into her house. Fred pocketed the money, retrieved the four sticks of well dried and solid, long burning hardwood and drove off. As he drove away he muttered to himself, "Well, I guess the customer is always right!!! From then on he always took only "good-looking" poplar and birch wood to Miss Ettie.

The road roller, or how not to deal with winter snow

In a museum in Washington D.C there hangs an early American painting of a large road roller being pulled by a team of horses along a country road. The device was made of wood and was perhaps 8 feet in diameter. I seriously doubt that Fred ever saw that painting or even knew of its existence, but the road roller that Fred described must have been similar to the one in that painting.

Getting from place to place in Vermont has always been a problem-- and it still is, at least for much of the year. When the snow falls in Vermont it's not like down in Massachusetts. When the snow falls in Vermont, it stays put. Not only that, when the snow falls in

Vermont, it keeps coming! Before long you've not only got snow, you've got plenty of it! And in Vermont you know that once you've got plenty snow, its going to be there, and its going to be there plenty long!

According to Fred the gravel road which passes near my house as it runs down the side of the mountain was once the main post road between Brattleboro and Bennington, Vermont. The road was rather heavily used by the local farmers and by many of the local mills and industries. Keeping the road open and clear of snow was a difficult job. Nowadays we've got fancy machines with powerful engines to help with the snow-- snowplows and snow blowers, and sanders and salters-- and we can put up quite a fight! In fact, nowadays for the most part in wintertime in Vermont you can actually get from place to place-- so long as those places are on one of the main roads

But when Fred was growing up, things were not so easy. When the snow fell it generally stayed there. Moving it off a road meant shovels, or horse power, or simple resignation! Horse drawn plows were slow and not very efficient. But the road needed to be kept open and people needed to get about. Horses can handle more snow than a man can, and horses could pull sleds loaded with goods-- but even horses move slow though heavy snow.

Fred did not remember who came up with the idea, but one winter genius struck in southern Vermont, and everyone seemed to agree that it was an idea good enough to be given a try. This fellow decided that not only was it a lot of trouble to move snow around, but that it was relatively easy to walk on snow once it had been packed down a little. Once the snow was packed down a man didn't need snowshoes, and the horses could make a pretty good clip, even pulling a loaded sled. Leaving the snow for the horses to pack down didn't work very well. Being smarter than most men, the horses tended to follow close in the track the first horse made, so the packed down trails generally stayed fairly narrow. Even a country genius could soon figure out that a narrow trail meant slow going for a full size and heavily laden sled

One winter when the first heavy snow fell (and Fred assured me of the fact that more snow fell in those days than what we now have to put up with!), the plan was put into action. This neighbor's answer to the problem was to build a snow roller. This invention of his was a heavy wooden roller pulled by a team of horses. The contraption was brought out and was pulled over this stretch of road to compact the snow. In no time at all the job was finished, and all the folks thereabout were delighted to be able to travel the road easily. Time and time again that winter the snow fell. And time and time again the road roller made short work of the problem and traveling to and from town <u>was</u> easier. You can be sure that the fellow, whoever he was, who dreamed up this idea was feeling pretty smug.

Now even in Vermont winter does finally come to an end. In Vermont when winter ends it is replaced by an even more unpleasant season: "Mud Season." First the snow melts, then the ground thaws, then all of the dry land turns to mud. Unfortunately our genius hadn't counted on Spring, or "Mud Season", coming to Vermont. Not that its so hard to understand this small mistake, because winter in Vermont always seems to last forever. But Springtime does eventually come even in Vermont, and this year was no exception. What was an exception, though, was what happened to the post road. Eventually the maple sap rose, the sun came out and the snow commenced to melt. Ice takes longer to melt, especially large blocks of ice. The compacted snow tried to melt, but it simply thawed partially, then froze solid into a giant block of ice several feet thick and several miles long! Horses, even wagons and buckboards, can travel rather easily and securely on packed snow, but a solid sheet of ice is another matter altogether. Once the Spring thaw began, travel on the road became impossible.

The problem didn't stop there. Melting snow in Vermont does two things: it breeds black flies, and it breeds mud! And when they say "mud" in Vermont, they mean real mud! The "Mud Season" arrived also, but for the first time anybody could remember there was no mud on the post road-- right up through the end of June! Unfortunately that didn't mean the road could be traveled, and with that big block of ice covering the road up and down the side of the mountain, travel on the road came to a standstill. When the snow melted in the fields, a few smart folks had the idea, "Let's pull off and go up along side the road." But that idea didn't last very long . Have you ever seen a wagon mired up to its axle in mud? The more people who tried to make their way through the mud, the deeper and stickier it became.

Somehow folks made it through that Spring, but the snow roller didn't. Folks suspected that it had been used to fire up somebody's maple sugar house to boil down the sap at sugaring time. Fred assured me that this grand idea was abandoned after that one winter and was never tried again. And, Fred asked, is it any wonder that no one seemed to take credit for the idea!

The shiny new "modern" fire truck

The folks in town in those days prided themselves on being progressive, up to date, and "modern." After all there were a number of mills, lime kilns, iron foundries, and other light manufacturing in the valley. Indeed the towns of Wilmington and Whitingham each had its own town hall, its own school and even a library. This corner of Vermont was becoming more prosperous, and folks were feeling pretty progressive.

However, the fire department had not been modernized and certainly was not up to big city standards. It was not just that the fire department was purely a volunteer undertaking. That part worked very well.

When the fire bell sounded at the town hall, many able bodied citizens were quick to respond. Folks stopped what they were doing and rushed to the firehouse. Often the barber put down his razor, and both he and a half-shaved customer would show up. Having enough people willing to help wasn't the problem. The problem was that many of the town's dwellings were situated on the side of the mountains with no lake or pond nearby to supply water, and most were constructed of wood. The venerable old fire wagon had to be hitched to a team of horses in order to respond to a fire. The wagon itself did not hold much water, and the water had to be propelled through the fire hose by a hand pump. That was tiring work- and it would have been even more tiring if the fire wagon had really held enough water to get the job done

One day the town fathers learned that a new and modern, gasoline powered fire truck was being sold in New York and was being used in the big cities. The fire truck carried a large tank of water and boasted a powerful pump to propel the water through its hose. Being self-propelled there was no need to take time to hitch up a team of horses. The fire truck was expensive, but the town fathers agreed that the expense might be justified. They decided to ask the manufacturer for a demonstration

The day chosen for the demonstration proved to be a warm and sunny one. Not only the townspeople, but people from all around showed up for the big day. There were gasps of admiration galore when the mighty fire truck chugged into town. It was painted bright red with brass fittings, and the engine gave out a loud and manly roar. It had a large tank which could be filled with water and had a long hose with a brass nozzle. The polished brass and the shiny red paint gleamed in the bright sunlight, and folks could just tell by looking at it that this was modern technology at its best!

The town selectmen took turns learning how to drive the mighty fire truck and roaring about the town, up and down the mountainside roads. Everyone seemed to be having a great time and a festive air prevailed. Water was put in the tank, and each fireman took a turn at directing the forceful stream of water put out by the fire hose. The water easily reached even the roofs of the nearby houses. By the end of the afternoon the volunteer firemen were pretty wet and they were tired, but they were elated. The town selectmen convened a special meeting. By unanimous vote they agreed to purchase the fire truck, despite its rather hefty price. The fire truck became the property of the town then and there, on the spot

Unfortunately disaster struck a few days later. A barn caught fire high on the mountainside. The fire truck was ready. Its tank had been filled to capacity with water. The gas tank was full. The engine leaped to life immediately with a loud roar. Several volunteer firemen responded immediately and climbed aboard the truck. Accompanied by the cheers of the firemen and several bystanders, the majestic fire truck rolled out of its garage. It rolled downhill for several hundred yards then turned to climb the steep road up the mountainside. But, to the consternation of all, it gradually came to a halt and the engine stalled. Several times the engine was restarted, but each time the fire truck was unable to climb the road! The firemen got off and tried to push- but to no avail! They turned the fire truck around, and it easily rumbled along the more level stretch of road. On the day of the demonstration, the fire truck had easily climbed that same steep road- but there had been no water in the tank at the time! A hurried consultation and heated debate ensued. If they drained the water out of the tank, the fire truck could make it to the scene of the fire, but there would be no water available to fight the fire! Finally a painful decision was reached. A team of horses was hitched to the fire truck and a dejected group of firemen arrived at the scene of the fire in time to douse the last embers from the destroyed building with a mighty stream of water propelled through the new fire hose with its shiny brass nozzle.

How to keep from freezing while plowing snow

High technology did eventually come to the Wilmington-Whitingham Valley in Vermont. For years the local residents had struggled to keep their roads open in the winter, but horse drawn plow equipment was slow and not very effective. When high technology arrived, it came in the form of one of the first ever motor driven snowplows to be manufactured. This imposing and magnificent machine had large open iron wheels with studs to grip the snow. The engine was loud and clangy, and it produced quite an output of hot exhaust. In front was a V-shaped snowplow which cleared the snow to both sides of the road at once. It was certainly powerful enough to do the job, even up and down the mountain roads. But just because it was powerful didn't mean that it was fast. In fact, at its top speed, it could easily have been passed by a horse drawn wagon.

When the first snows fell, the town employees all were eager to drive this magnificent contraption, and they even had to take turns doing so. They certainly received a lot of attention from the townspeople, farmers and dairymen when they came chugging along pushing and blowing snow off of both sides at once. And it was certainly grand to have the roads open and free of snow!

In Vermont, as winter progresses the mercury has a way of falling in the thermometers as the temperature dips to levels appropriately referred to as "bitter cold." On those days of extreme cold when snow plowing was called for, one of the limitations of the new machine became increasingly apparent. In order for the driver to see over the big V-shaped plow blade, the driver sat high up on the contraption. The seat was made of steel -- and steel can get cold in cold weather -- and no one had thought to mount it on springs. Furthermore, even though there was a small roof over the driver's seat, there were no panels on either side, front or back. This left the driver with a completely unobstructed view, but it also left him completely exposed to the howling wind and blowing snow. Staying warm became an important concern, and the town workers preferred to keep from freezing or even from getting frost bitten. Not surprisingly, the enthusiasm for driving the magnificent snowplow gradually began to wane.

Finally, Vermont ingenuity came to the rescue of high technology. The snowplow was a very steady machine, so much so that it took some force to turn the steering wheel.

Consequently, once the machine was set on course on a straight stretch of road, it tended to continue to plow along on a straight line. Faced with impending frostbite, one of the town workers hit upon a happy solution. Each time he came to a straight stretch of road, he put the snowplow in its lowest gear, reducing its speed to little more than a brisk crawl. He would then hop down off of the high and cold metal driver's seat and step around behind the moving vehicle. The large exhaust pipe came out just about at waist level, and it continually belched hot exhaust fumes. By walking along behind the snowplow and rubbing his hands together just behind the exhaust pipe, the plow driver could actually keep himself fairly comfortable! Fortunately, walking along behind the clanging machine insured that the driver stayed awake, but it was necessary for him to keep an eye ahead for any approaching curves in the road.

But for a nail a road was lost

In bygone days iron nails were often cut by hand, and in any case they were expensive. Construction was often done with wooden pegs hammered into holes drilled by hand, but this was time consuming and therefore was expensive also. Gradually the use of iron nails replaced the use of wooden pegs, but iron nails remained a premium item. On the farm near where my house now stands there once stood a finely constructed barn. The barn was painted bright red and was solidly built. Iron nails had been used throughout the entire construction. It was a two story affair, with stalls for the animals on the ground floor and a hayloft above. It took a lot of nails to build that barn. That barn was certainly the farmer's pride.

Unfortunately one summer afternoon a thunderstorm came rolling through the area with flashing lightning and rolling thunder. One bolt of lightning struck the barn and set it on fire. The volunteer firemen came and did their best but it was too late. The barn burned to the ground. No farm animals were killed, but the barn was a total loss. Almost. The iron nails survived the fire and continued to have potential value.

One day not too long after the fire, the farmer and his wife went over the mountain to Brattleboro to meet with the insurance agent and the bank. It was a considerable trip in a horse drawn buckboard, so most folks who traveled that far allowed time to do most of their shopping while they were in the bigger town. News travels fast in a small and folksy community, and all the neighbors soon knew about the trip. Unfortunately a nere do well rascal who lived not too far away also learned that they would be away from home for the afternoon. He allowed that this seemed like a fine opportunity to make himself a little bit rich, with little likelihood of being caught in the process. He knew exactly where he could sell a fine passel of pre-used nails, and he grew thirstier just thinking about how he could spend the money. He laid his plans carefully. To avoid suspicion he walked through the woods to the scene of the fire carrying a wooden keg and tools to remove the nails. Quickly he picked up all of the loose nails and put them into his keg. The nails that were still imbedded in charred boards and timbers he removed and added to his hoard. He was not one who normally took kindly to hard work, but this was working for a purpose, so he went hard at it. Even though extracting the nails was hard and dirty labor, he had his thirst to give him strength and determination. More and more the keg filled with nails.

When he was nearly finished with his nefarious deed, he heard a wagon and team of horses nearing the top of the hill and heading over the top in his direction. By now the keg was nearly full of the iron nails and it was so heavy he could barely carry it. Not wanting to be caught in the act of stealing nails, he quickly looked about for a place to hide his loot. Nearby was a culvert under the road, which in those days was the post road and was rather heavily traveled. The culvert was just large enough for him to stash his heavy keg of nails. After doing so he quickly slipped away into the woods and made good his escape without being detected. All the way home he congratulated himself on his success and relished the thought, and taste-- of his anticipated reward. He planned to return that night with his own wagon and horses to retrieve the nails

Unfortunately the best laid plans often go awry, both good plans and evil plans. Along about nightfall the sky rapidly darkened. The black clouds rolled in, and the sun disappeared. Then the heavens opened up and a torrential downpour began. It rained for hour after hour. You would have thought the sky had saved up all summer for that rain, and it sure seemed to be trying to make up for lost time. It was a real toad strangler and a gully washer. With all that rain coming down it had to go somewhere, and it had to get there fast. The ditch alongside the road rapidly filled with rushing water, washing along sticks, leaves, stones and other debris.

When all that water reached the culvert, it found its way largely blocked by that heavy keg of nails, which refused to budge. As the debris piled up around the keg, the culvert became completely blocked. Now the water had nowhere to go except across the road. The rain didn't seem to mind what was happening to the road, and the water just kept coming down in buckets. Now a gravel road is not as secure as a macadam road, and it certainly isn't as good at taking water. With all that water rushing across the road, the gravel got washed along too. It didn't take long for the road to be completely washed out!

When people came the next day to inspect the damage, there was the incriminating keg of iron nails. The nails were washed clean and the dirty deed was laid bare. The rascal who stole the nails was never caught. But he lived on the other side of town across the road washout, and he too needed to use the road to get to town and to his work. His greed had not been rewarded, and in fact all he had succeeded in doing was to cut himself off from his livelihood--- and from the tavern where he usually slaked his thirst.

Old Doc works
a miracle

In the old days getting sick was a frightening and dangerous experience. "Old Doc" provided the best medical care he could, but he was the only doctor thereabouts. In those days and in rural Vermont there were no X-ray machines available, and only a few of the medicines which we now take for granted had been invented. Old Doc was a good doctor who cared deeply for his patients, and his patients loved him. But he would be one of the first to tell you that there were many diseases in the world which he could not cure, and diseases had won many of the grim battles which he had fought

In those days pneumonia was one of those diseases which often defied treatment and not uncommonly claimed the life of its victim. Unlike now, when pneumonia can usually be cured with antibiotics, in those days pneumonia was one of the dreaded diseases. Even young and healthy people unlucky enough to be striken with pneumonia became fevered, sickened, took to their beds, and all too often left their beds only after they had gasped their last breath.

One fateful day Fred awoke with a fever and a tightness in his chest. A few days before he had caught a bad cold from one of his children. As the day wore on his fever refused to break and that tightness in his chest grew stronger and more painful. Fred's wife grew more fearful, and Fred felt an awful foreboding. Along in the afternoon she bundled him into the family wagon and drove him into town to see Old Doc.

In his office Old Doc took Fred's temperature, looked at the thermometer, shook it a few times, then shook his head. Then he listened to Fred's chest with his well worn stethoscope and thumped around. He shook his head again. "Fred," he said, "I hate to tell you this, but I think you have pneumonia. I'm going to give you these pills, and I want you to take them and to follow my instructions very carefully. Take one of these pills each morning, then go out and cut and split two cords of wood. And don't forget to stack the wood! I'll check with you three days from now. "But Doc," Fred protested, "I'm so sick I feel weak as a dishrag! I can hardly get up and move, much less do any work, and my chest hurts every time I take a breath. How can you possibly expect me to cut, split and stack so much fire wood? That'll kill me for sure!"

Doc replied, "Fred, you're a strong man and you've been cutting firewood all your life. You can do it. And besides, its important for your treatment. You've always trusted me in the past, and most of the time I was right You've just got to trust me this time. Now go home and do exactly what I've told you."

The next morning, after a restless night, Fred awoke feeling terrible. His fever was raging, his chest hurt and he had trouble taking a deep breath. But Fred had faith in Old Doc, and he sure did want to get well and go on with his life. Just as Old Doc had told him to do he took the first pill. The pill was so big he could hardly swallow it, and it was colored bright red. He swallowed it down with a glass of water, but he didn't feel much like eating. After taking the pill he dragged himself out to the wood lot and began cutting firewood. It was laborious and painful work, but he trusted Old Doc and figured that he knew best. Being a determined and stubborn Vermonter he stuck with his task all day and finished about sunset. He was so exhausted he could hardly drag himself back into the house and flop down on the bed. His wife had fixed him a nourishing supper, but he didn't feel up to eating much. Even the children were quiet that evening. They knew that something was bad wrong, and they were frightened

That night Fred was so exhausted that he did sleep better, but again the next morning he awoke feeling just as terrible. Again his chest hurt and he had trouble breathing. He managed to swallow the second huge red pill with a glass of water and a few spoonfuls of oatmeal, then again he headed for the wood lot. Once again he struggled through a long and painful day, stopping frequently to try to catch his breath. Somehow once again he managed to complete his assigned therapy. Again he barely made it into his house and collapsed on the bed without eating much of the supper his wife had made. The children tried to get him to eat too, and they quickly fetched the few things he asked them to get.

Once again that night exhaustion helped Fred to sleep better. Unfortunately he awoke still feeling terrible. His chest still hurt and he still had trouble breathing. The third big red pill went down with a glass of butter milk. This morning the milk actually tasted good, and Fred felt slightly encouraged. With renewed determination he headed again for the wood lot and began to cut wood. Along about mid morning Fred felt something break loose in his chest and rattle around in his throat. He hawked and spat. Then he took a deep breath.

Then he took another, and it came easily and it felt good. He realized also that his fever had broken! With a great sense of relief and happiness he resumed his work with renewed vigor. Now the wood fairly flew and the ax seemed to be singing in the air. The stack of firewood rose far more rapidly today than it had on the two previous, tortured days.

Along about noon Old Doc came riding up in his buggy with his well-worn and somewhat tattered black bag on the seat beside him. Fred greeted him warmly and said, "Doc, you were right. You are indeed a blessing to this community and a wise doctor. I trusted you and did just what you told me-- and it sure has paid off. I feel like a new man! Those pills were wonderful and they certainly did the trick!"

Sitting up in his buggy Old Doc looked at the jubilant Fred and seemed right proud of himself. He grinned broadly, then broke out into a hearty laugh. He replied, "Aw shucks, Fred, those pills weren't nothing but sugar. It was the work that cured you. I just came over to see if you were alive or dead!"

Postlude

The "Good old days" in Vermont are now gone. Old Fred Bernard is gone also and his earthly remains are buried in the Vermont soil he loved so much, though quite likely Fred is still telling tall tales in an even better place. But part of Fred lives on. My memory of Fred lives on, as does my memory of the scenes Fred so vividly painted with his words. Vermont lives on too, as a land of beauty and tranquility (despite the incursion of snowmobiles and an increasing horde of vacation landowners) where a special breed of people still live. My family and I still come to Vermont to escape the bustle and noise of city life and the stress and hectic pace of a civilization driven by technology. I think of Fred often. His zest for life was infectious, and I am glad that he left behind such wonderful stories and fond memories. Fred's daughters recall that one of Fred's favorite sayings was, "Well, if you plant turnips. . . , you're going to get turnips!" This time, though, Fred planted words, and out of those words grew precious memories of the vivid and often humorous activites of some special people in the bygone days of Vermont.